To Joe.
For your cooking pleasure.
Marilyn Myers

FRESH MONTHLY

Menus From

AUGUST HOUSE

AUGUST HOUSE, INC., Publishers
1010 West Third Street
Little Rock, Arkansas 72201
(501) 376-4516

Because of
Beth Fair

With a special thanks to
Sally Manesberg Flanzer

Illustrations by Louise Terzia

Copyright 1981 by Marilyn Myers.
Published 1981 by August House, Inc.,
1010 West Third Street, Little Rock, AR 72201.
(501) 376-4516

First Printing, May 1981

Library of Congress Catalog Card No.:
    80-65462
    Myers, Marilyn
    Fresh Monthly: Menus from
    Little Rock: August House

CONTENTS

JANUARY   5
Dinner for six

Beef Burgundy
Buttered potatoes
Grand Marnier soufflé
Gamay Beaujolais

FEBRUARY   9
Supper for six

Purée of carrot soup with cabbage
Country white bread
Chocolate Bavarian cream
Johannisberg Riesling

MARCH   15
Dinner for four

Roast chicken with sautéed cherry
   tomatoes
Potato puffs
Pineapple with apricot sauce
Pinot Noir Blanc

APRIL   21
Luncheon for four

Vichyssoise
Artichokes stuffed with lump
   crabmeat
Crêpes Suzette
Dry Chenin Blanc

MAY   27
Supper for six

Cucumber and yogurt soup
Spring salad
Angel food cake with strawberry
   sauce
White table wine

JUNE   33
Dinner for six

Chicken in lemon sauce
Tomatoes Nicoise
Blueberry tart
Chardonnay

JULY   39
Supper for four

Green pepper salad
Cheese soufflé
Frozen raspberry mousse
Zinfandel

AUGUST   43
Dinner for four

Black pepper steak
Potato salad with string beans
Peaches in peach cream sauce
Cabernet Sauvignon

SEPTEMBER   47
Dinner for six

Roast pork stuffed with prunes
Pan-roasted potatoes and carrots
Apple Charlotte
Sauvignon Blanc

OCTOBER   51
Dinner for six

Beef Stroganoff
Egg noodles
Pears with chocolate sauce
Pinot Noir

NOVEMBER   55
Dinner for six

Scallops in cream sauce with rice
Bibb lettuce salad
Rolled chocolate cake
Dry Chablis

DECEMBER   61
Supper for four

Oyster stew
Yeast rolls
Plum pudding with hard sauce
Brut Champagne

Foods are best when fresh and in season.

This book follows the monthly changes and mood of the market in a variety of menus that cover a wide selection of classic recipes. The dishes in each menu are designed to compliment each other. An appropriate wine selection is offered also.

I hope you enjoy *Fresh Monthly*.

Marilyn Myers
February, 1981

January Menu

Beef Burgundy
Buttered potatoes
Grand Marnier soufflé

Gamay Beaujolais

Dinner for six

Beef Burgundy is a classic winter recipe for good reason. It is a refined dish; it uses ingredients readily available in the market; and it
is guaranteed to satisfy a cold weather appetite. The buttered
potatoes add extra nourishment to the meal and the Grand Marnier
soufflé finishes the dinner on a delicate note.

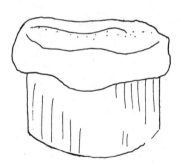

Beef Burgundy

2½ pounds beef chuck or shank
2 tablespoons peanut oil
2 tablespoons cognac
3 tablespoons all-purpose flour
3 cups red wine
1-2 cups water
½ cup tomato purée
4 small garlic cloves, crushed
salt and freshly ground black pepper
bouquet garni of
    pinch of thyme
    1 bay leaf
    4 parsley sprigs
½ pound salt pork
12 tiny white pearl onions
    or 4 small yellow onions, quartered
6 medium carrots, carved into olive shapes
½ pound mushrooms, trimmed and sliced

1. Trim the fat and gristle from the meat and cut into 1-inch cubes. Dry the meat on paper towels.

2. Heat the oil in a large heavy-bottomed casserole, add a portion of the meat, and brown it on all sides over medium high heat. Do not crowd the meat in the pan. When the meat has browned, remove it to a side plate and continue with the remaining pieces.

3. Return all the meat to the pan, add the cognac, and scrape the bottom of the casserole with a wooden spoon.

4. Add the flour, stirring the meat around to coat it. Cook over medium heat about 5 minutes or until the flour is lightly browned.

5. Add the wine and enough water to barely cover the meat. Add the tomato purée, the garlic cloves, salt and pepper, and bouquet garni. Bring to a boil, then reduce the heat to a simmer and cook, covered, for 1½-2 hours or until the meat is tender but firm. Skim any fat and foam off the surface of the sauce several times during this period and stir gently so that meat and flour do not attach to the bottom of the pan.

6. Remove the rind from the salt pork and cut into small cubes. Drop in boiling water for 3 minutes. Drain.

7. Place the cubes of salt pork in a sauté pan over medium heat and cook until a little of the fat is rendered. Add the onions to the pan and continue cooking until the salt pork is golden and crispy and the onion is lightly browned. Remove the salt pork and onion with a slotted spoon and discard the fat.

8. Remove the meat from the casserole and pass the sauce through a fine sieve into a clean bowl. Return the sauce to the casserole and add the meat, salt pork, onions, and carrots. Cook for 45 minutes.

9. Add the mushrooms and cook for 15 minutes. The beef Burgundy may be held at this point. Reheat slowly before serving.

Buttered Potatoes

12 small all-purpose potatoes
6 tablespoons butter
salt and freshly ground white pepper
2 tablespoons finely minced parsley

1. Scrub the potatoes thoroughly. If the potatoes are different sizes, trim so that they are uniform but no smaller than a jumbo egg.

2. Bring a large saucepan of water to a boil and add 1 teaspoon salt. Add the potatoes and cook uncovered about 20 minutes or until the potatoes are tender when pierced with a fork.

3. Drain the potatoes, rinse quickly with cold water, and peel off the skins when cool enough to handle.

4. Melt the butter in a large sauté pan. Add the potatoes and let them dry out over medium heat for a few minutes.

5. Toss the potatoes in the pan to coat evenly with butter. Season with salt and pepper, sprinkle with parsley, and toss again.

Grand Marnier Soufflé

5 eggs, separated
⅓ cup granulated sugar
finely grated rind of 1 medium orange
¼ cup Grand Marnier
1 tablespoon confectioners' sugar

1. Put the egg yolks in a bowl and gradually stir in the sugar, beating until the batter is thick and a light yellow color.

2. Blend in the grated orange rind and the Grand Marnier.

3. Preheat the oven to 400 degrees. Butter a 6-cup soufflé dish and dust with granulated sugar.

4. Beat the egg whites in a copper or stainless steel bowl until they are glossy and stiff. Do not beat so long that they dry out.

5. Pour the batter over the egg whites. Fold in just until blended. It is better to leave small clumps of egg whites than to overwork the mixture.

6. Pour the mixture into the soufflé dish and bake in the oven for 12 minutes. To test if it is done, give the dish a slight shove. If the top crust moves slightly it is ready; if it trembles cook 3-4 minutes longer.

7. Remove from the oven and sieve the confectioners' sugar over the top. The soufflé must be served immediately. It will have a creamy center.

February Menu

Purée of carrot soup with cabbage
Country white bread
Chocolate Bavarian cream

Johannisberg Riesling

Supper for six

A sagging February spirit can be effectively countered by a hearty soup and bread fresh from the oven. The subtle flavor of carrots and potatoes in the soup provides a fine base for the stronger statement of another popular winter vegetable, cabbage. The country bread contributes to the wholesome quality of the meal; the chocolate Bavarian cream is sheer indulgence.

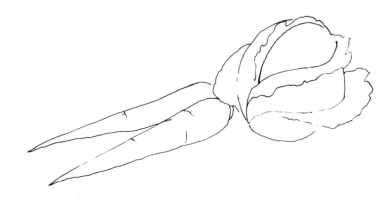

Purée Of Carrot Soup With Cabbage

3 tablespoons butter
1 medium onion, finely diced
1 small green cabbage, finely shredded into
    approximately 2-inch lengths
4 medium carrots, diced
2 medium all-purpose potatoes, diced
2 teaspoons salt
6 cups water
    or 3 cups water and 3 cups chicken stock
1 teaspoon dry dill
salt and freshly ground white pepper
1 cup sour cream

1. Using a large saucepan or stockpot, sauté the onion in 1 tablespoon of butter over medium heat about 5 minutes until limp but not browned. Add the cabbage, 1 teaspoon salt, and 3 cups water. Bring to a boil and simmer uncovered 10-15 minutes until the cabbage is tender. Remove from the heat.

2. Place the carrots, potatoes, 1 teaspoon salt, and 3 cups water or chicken stock in a separate saucepan and bring to a boil. Simmer for 10-15 minutes until the vegetables are tender.

3. Drain the water or stock from the potatoes and carrots into the pot with the cabbage. Pass the potato/carrot mixture through a food mill or ricer or whip with a potato masher.

4. Thoroughly blend the remaining 2 tablespoons of butter and the dill into the puréed vegetables and then stir this into the cabbage mixture. The soup may be held at this point until ready for service.

5. Reheat the soup and season with salt and pepper if necessary. Stir the sour cream into the soup at the last moment, mixing well. Do not let the soup boil once the sour cream has been added.

Country White Bread

2 packages yeast
2 cups warm water
5½-6½ cups bread flour
1 tablespoon salt

GLAZE
1 egg
2 tablespoons warm water
pinch of salt

1. Add the yeast to ½ cup warm water (80-90 degrees for compressed yeast, 110-115 for dry). Let it soften for a few minutes, then stir to dissolve.

2. Place 3 cups of flour, salt, and 1½ cups warm water in a large mixing bowl. Add the yeast and beat with a wooden spoon until the mixture is free of lumps.

3. Add 2½ more cups of flour and mix, with a wooden spoon and then with the hands, until a rough dough is formed. If the dough is too sticky at this point, work in just enough flour until the dough can be handled.

4. Turn the dough out onto a lightly floured work surface and knead for 10-15 minutes. When necessary, dust the work surface with additional flour to keep the dough from sticking.

5. When the dough is very springy and smooth, place it in a lightly buttered, large mixing bowl. Turn it over and around so that all sides are coated with butter, cover the bowl with plastic wrap, and place in a warm spot to let the dough rise until doubled in bulk. At about 85 degrees, the dough will double in 1-1½ hours.

6. Punch down the dough and fold the edges into the center of the dough. Turn the dough over, cover with plastic wrap, and let rise again in a warm spot until doubled in bulk. The second rising should take 45-60 minutes.

7. Punch down the dough, turn it out onto a work surface, and knead lightly for 2-3 minutes. Divide the dough into two pieces, cover with plastic wrap, and let the dough rest 10 minutes.

8. Line a large baking sheet with cooking parchment paper. Shape each piece of dough into a rectangle about 2 inches shorter than the sheet. Fold the long sides over each other and tuck in the ends. Further shape the dough by rolling it back and forth on the work surface using the palms of the hands.

9. To glaze the bread, beat the egg and salted water in a small bowl and lightly brush the mixture on the surface of the loaves. Slash the loaves three times on the diagonal, using a very sharp knife or razor blade and going about ⅛-inch deep. Let the loaves rise 30-45 minutes or until they have doubled in size.

10. Preheat the oven to 425 degrees and bake the loaves for 15 minutes. Turn the heat to 350 degrees and continue baking 25-30 minutes. The loaves are done when the bottom crust has browned nicely and sounds hollow when tapped. Cool on a wire rack before slicing.

Chocolate Bavarian Cream

2 cups whole milk
1 vanilla bean*
8 eggs yolks
⅔ cup granulated sugar
1 tablespoon (4 sheets) unflavored gelatin
6 ounces semisweet baking chocolate, broken in pieces
1¼ cups heavy whipping cream
2 teaspoons confectioners' sugar

1. Put the milk and vanilla bean in a heavy-bottomed saucepan over medium heat, bring to a boil, and remove from the heat.

2. Place the egg yolks in a mixing bowl and beat in the sugar. Continue beating until the mixture is a pale yellow color.

3. Slowly stir the milk into the beaten eggs. Do not remove the vanilla bean.

4. Clean the saucepan and pour the mixture into it. Cook the custard 10-15 minutes over low heat until it thickens. Stir constantly with a wooden spoon, making sure that it touches the bottom of the pan. The surface foam and air bubbles will disappear, and when the spoon is lifted out of the sauce only a drop or two will fall from it. Do not let the custard boil or the eggs will curdle.

5. Remove from the heat and take out the vanilla bean. Add the chocolate and stir until well blended.

6. Soften the gelatin in 3 tablespoons of cold water (or soak the gelatin sheets in enough water to cover for 5 minutes, then squeeze out the excess moisture). Stir the gelatin into the hot sauce, being sure it dissolves.

7. Pass the sauce through a fine sieve into a clean bowl. Place a piece of plastic wrap on the surface of the sauce and set it in the refrigerator for 30-60 minutes until it has completely cooled.

8. Whip the cream in a stainless steel bowl until it begins to stiffen and forms soft peaks.

9. Fold the whipped cream into the chocolate custard, making sure that it is well blended. Pour the Bavarian cream into a 6-cup mold that has been rinsed in cold water. Let it set up in the refrigerator 3-4 hours.

10. To serve, dip the mold in hot water for a second or two and unmold onto a serving plate. Sieve confectioners' sugar over the top.

*If a vanilla bean is unavailable, add 2 teaspoons of vanilla extract just before blending in the chocolate in step 5.

March Menu

Roast chicken with sautéed cherry tomatoes
Potato puffs
Pineapple with apricot sauce

Pinot Noir Blanc

Dinner for four

March, with its promise of Spring, suggests a graceful touch at the dinner table. The roast chicken is pleasantly seasoned and brightened with the addition of sautéed cherry tomatoes. The potato puffs are light and breezy. Pineapple — at its peak — is the sunny finale.

Roast Chicken With Sautéed Cherry Tomatoes

1 four-pound chicken
salt and freshly ground white pepper
½ teaspoon paprika
½ teaspoon dried marjoram
1 small garlic clove, crushed
1 teaspoon Dijon mustard
4 tablespoons butter
1 large carrot, diced
1 medium onion, diced
1 celery rib, diced
1 cup dry white wine
¼ cup heavy whipping cream
1 pint cherry tomatoes
2 tablespoons olive oil
1 teaspoon granulated sugar
1 tablespoon finely minced parsley

1. Preheat the oven to 400 degrees.

2. Dry the chicken cavity and season with salt and pepper. Truss the chicken and wipe the outside. Using a mortar and pestle, grind the salt, pepper, paprika, and marjoram with the garlic clove. Blend in the mustard. Rub the chicken skin with this paste.

3. Melt the butter in a roasting pan big enough to snugly hold the chicken. Sauté the diced vegetables over medium heat 3-4 minutes and add 1 cup of white wine.

4. Place the chicken on top of the vegetables and roast in the oven for 10 minutes. Turn the heat to 375 degrees, baste the chicken, and cook at this temperature 80-90 minutes. Baste every 20 minutes during the roasting. If the chicken is browning too quickly, cover the bird loosely with aluminum foil. To test if the chicken is done, prick the thickest part of the thigh with a kitchen fork. The juice that flows should be quite clear with no trace of pink.

5. When the chicken is done remove it from the pan and pass the pan juices through a sieve, pressing out the liquid from the vegetables. Skim off the fat and discard. Combine this liquid with the cream in a saucepan and, over low heat, reduce the sauce until it begins to thicken.

6. While the sauce is simmering, add the cherry tomatoes to the olive oil in a hot sauté pan. Sprinkle with sugar and freshly ground white pepper and cook over medium heat until the tomatoes just begin to wilt. Immediately put the tomatoes in a serving dish and sprinkle with parsley.

7. Remove the trussing from the chicken and transfer to a serving platter. Coat the chicken with a small amount of sauce. Pass the remaining sauce and the cherry tomatoes at table.

Potato Puffs

½ pound all-purpose potatoes
½ cup water
2 tablespoons butter
¼ teaspoon salt
½ cup all-purpose flour
2 eggs
4-6 cups peanut oil
salt

1. Peel the potatoes and cook in boiling, salted water for about 20 minutes or until tender. Pass the potatoes through a food mill or ricer or whip with a potato masher.

2. Place the water, butter, and salt in a heavy-bottomed saucepan. When the butter has melted and the water is boiling, remove from the heat and add the flour all at once, mixing rapidly with a wooden spoon until a dough forms.

3. Over low heat, dry the dough for 5-6 minutes, pushing it back and forth from one side of the pan to the other. The dough will become shiny and will not cling to the wooden spoon. Transfer the dough to a clean bowl. Do not scrape out the thin crust on the bottom of the pan. Let the dough cool for 5 minutes.

4. Beat in the eggs, one at a time. Be sure that the mixture is smooth and shiny after each addition.

5. Mix the mashed potatoes with the egg dough. There should be 1 cup of each.

6. Heat the peanut oil in a deep skillet or frying pan to 340 degrees. The oil should be at least 1-inch deep.

7. Push the dough into the hot oil by teaspoonfuls, getting as close to the oil as possible to avoid a splash. Cook for 8-10 minutes. Allow for the dough to expand and do not crowd the pan.

8. Drain the potato puffs on paper towels and salt lightly. They may be held briefly on a cooling rack in a 150-degree oven.

Pineapple With Apricot Sauce

1 large pineapple
1 lemon
2 cups water
1 cup granulated sugar
½ vanilla bean
¾ cup dried apricots
2 tablespoons light rum

1. Cut off both ends of the pineapple and trim away the outer rind. Cut in quarters and remove the core from each section. Cut the pineapple in cubes.

2. Using a vegetable peeler, remove the very outer, yellow portion of the lemon in long strips. Squeeze the juice of half the lemon into a small bowl.

3. Put the water and sugar in a heavy-bottomed saucepan over low heat. Stir until the sugar has dissolved, then brush down the sides of the pan with water. Add the vanilla bean, lemon rind and juice, and simmer for 5 minutes.

4. Add the pineapple and simmer, covered, for 5 minutes. Remove the pineapple from the saucepan with a slotted spoon.

5. Add the dried apricots to the syrup and simmer uncovered for 30 minutes.

6. Remove the vanilla bean and lemon rind and pass the stewed apricots and syrup through a food mill and then a fine sieve. Stir in the light rum. If necessary, reduce the sauce over medium heat until it is the consistency of heavy cream.

7. Transfer the pineapple to a serving dish, pour the sauce over it, and chill for 1 hour.

*If a vanilla bean is unavailable, add 1 teaspoon of vanilla extract along with the rum in step 6.

April Menu

Vichyssoise
Artichokes stuffed with lump crabmeat
Crêpes Suzette

Dry Chenin Blanc

Luncheon for four

Spring onions are in fully glory in April yards, filling the air with their distinctive aroma. It is a perfect time to enjoy the leek — that mild and sweet branch of the onion family — in an elegant vichyssoise. With the tone of the meal set, the artichoke filled with lump crabmeat and crêpes Suzette are naturals to follow.

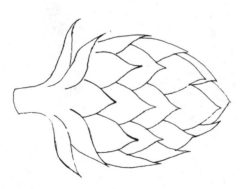

Vichyssoise

2 medium leeks
1 small onion
2 medium all-purpose potatoes
2 tablespoons butter
2 cups chicken stock or water
salt and freshly ground white pepper
2 cups half and half
1 cup whole milk
1 tablespoon chopped chives

1. Trim the green portion off the leeks. Starting ¼ inch from the root end, cut each leek in quarters. Thoroughly rinse the leeks in cold water to remove all sand. Dice into ½-inch cubes.

2. Dice the onions. Peel and dice the potatoes.

3. Melt the butter in a large saucepan and simmer the leeks and onions for 3-5 minutes until they are limp but not brown.

4. Add the chicken stock or water and potatoes. Add salt and pepper and simmer the soup for 30 minutes or until the potatoes are tender.

5. Pass the soup through a food mill.

6. Return the soup to the saucepan and add the half and half and milk. Heat almost to the boiling point, stirring often.

7. Pass the soup through a fine sieve into a clean bowl. Taste and correct the seasoning. Place in the refrigerator at least 8 hours until thoroughly chilled. Transfer the soup to a serving bowl or tureen and garnish the soup with chopped chives.

Artichokes Stuffed With Lump Crabmeat

4 large artichokes
juice of 1 lemon
½ pound lump crabmeat
⅔ cup mayonnaise*
2 teaspoons Dijon mustard
1 tablespoon diced pimiento
¼ teaspoon paprika
salt and freshly ground white pepper

GARNISH
1 medium head bibb or Boston lettuce
4 hard-cooked eggs

1. Cut the stems of the artichokes off at the base and pull away any dry leaves.

2. Cut 1½ inches off the top of the artichoke. Rub both the top and bottom cut surfaces with a little of the lemon juice.

3. Put the artichokes in boiling, salted water. Add all but 2 teaspoons of the lemon juice to the water also. Cook the artichokes 30-40 minutes or until tender. If a leaf at the base of the artichoke pulls off easily, it is done.

4. Drain the artichokes, upside down, on paper towels.

5. Pick over the crabmeat to remove any bones and place in a mixing bowl.

6. Blend together the mayonnaise, the remaining 2 teaspoons of lemon juice, mustard, pimiento, paprika, salt, and pepper. Add the crabmeat and mix well. Both the artichokes and the crabmeat filling may be held at this point.

7. Gently spread the inside leaves of the artichokes just enough to get at the very center leaves. Pull these leaves out to expose the fuzzy choke. Remove the choke with the tip of a spoon.

8. Fill the artichokes with the crabmeat. Serve the artichokes on a plate lined with rinsed and trimmed lettuce surrounded by quartered hard-cooked eggs.

*Directions for a mayonnaise are given in the recipe for Spring salad, steps 8-10.

Crêpes Suzette

CREPES
¾ cup milk
3 eggs
½ cup all-purpose flour
2 teaspoons granulated sugar
1 tablespoon orange liqueur
4 tablespoons butter, clarified*

ORANGE BUTTER
8 tablespoons butter, softened
¼ cup granulated sugar
1 orange rind, grated
2 tablespoons orange liqueur

SYRUP
6 sugar cubes, rubbed over an orange rind
¾ cup granulated sugar
1 orange
6 tablespoons butter
½ cup orange liqueur
3 tablespoons cognac

CREPES
1. Place the milk, eggs, flour, and sugar in a mixing bowl and whisk until the batter is free of lumps. Pass the mixture through a fine sieve and blend in the orange liqueur and 1 tablespoon of the clarified butter.

2. Brush the surface of the crêpe pan with a very small amount of the clarified butter. Place the pan over medium heat and when hot add 2 tablespoons of batter to the pan, turning the pan around in a smooth motion so that the batter is evenly distributed over the surface. If the batter does not cover the bottom of the pan easily, blend in a little more milk.

3. Cook the crêpe 2-3 minutes until the bottom side is lightly browned. Loosen and turn over with the fingers. Cook on the other side 30-60 seconds. Turn out onto a plate. Lightly brush the pan with butter after every other crêpe. Put a piece of wax paper between the crêpes as they are stacked. Covered with foil, the crêpe will hold in a 200-degree oven for about 30 minutes. They may also be refrigerated and reheated in foil in the oven.

ORANGE BUTTER

4. Beat the butter until it is light and fluffy.

5. Gradually beat in the granulated sugar, the orange rind, and the orange liqueur. The orange butter may be held in the refrigerator.

6. Just before serving time, bring the orange butter to room temperature. Spread the less attractive side of the crêpes with a portion of the orange butter and fold the crêpe in half, and half again, making a triangle. Hold on wax paper.

SYRUP AND FINAL ASSEMBLING

7. Using a vegetable peeler, remove the very outer, dark portion of the orange in strips. Cut these strips into long slivers. Squeeze the juice of the orange into a small bowl.

8. Place the sugar cubes, granulated sugar, orange slivers and juice, butter, and ⅓ cup of the orange liqueur in a flambéing or frying pan. Cook over medium heat until the orange rind has softened and the liquid is syrupy.

9. Warm the remaining orange liqueur and cognac in a small saucepan.

10. Arrange the crêpes in a circle around the flambéing or frying pan. Spoon the sauce over them.

11. Pour the warmed liqueurs over the crêpes and ignite with a kitchen match. Shake the pan to distribute the flame. Serve as soon as the fire has died.

*For a description of clarified butter, see step 2 of the recipe for rolled chocolate cake.

May Menu

Cucumber and yogurt soup
Spring salad
Angel food cake with strawberry sauce

White table wine

Supper for six

A Spring salad delights the senses and brings much of the seasonal bounty to the table. Asparagus, new potatoes, watercress, and avocados are all plentiful, and this attractive presentation shows them at their best. The cucumber and yogurt soup is a refreshing beginning for the meal. The angel food cake, with fresh strawberries in the sauce, is a perfect May ending.

Cucumber And Yogurt Soup

2 medium cucumbers
1 small garlic clove
3½ cups plain yogurt
1-2 cups heavy whipping cream
¾ cup golden raisins
1 tablespoon fresh dill
*   or 1 teaspoon dry dill*
salt and freshly ground white pepper

1. Peel the cucumbers. Cut off and discard the ends, cut in half lengthwise, and scoop out the seeds. Grate the cucumbers and place in a sieve to drain, pressing out the water with the back of a spoon.

2. Peel and crush the garlic clove. Place it and ¼ teaspoon salt in a mortar and grind with a pestle until a paste is formed.

3. Put the garlic paste, yogurt, 1 cup of cream, the raisins, and dill in a bowl and stir until well blended.

4. Taste and season with pepper and additional salt, if necessary. Chill 1 hour before serving in order to plump the raisins. The soup will thicken as it sits. It may be necessary to stir in a portion of the remaining cream before serving.

Spring Salad

SALAD
6 tiny new potatoes
12 asparagus stalks
2 eggs
1 large head romaine lettuce
1 bunch watercress
12 medium mushrooms
1 medium avocado
juice of half a lemon
1 ounce (1 cup) alfalfa sprouts
6 black olives
6 cherry tomatoes, halved

MAYONNAISE DRESSING
1 egg yolk
salt and freshly ground white pepper
2 teaspoons Dijon mustard
1 tablespoon lemon juice
¾-1 cup peanut oil
¼-⅓ cup heavy whipping cream
¼ teaspoon paprika

SALAD
1. Cook the potatoes in boiling, salted water for 7-12 minutes or just until tender. Cool under running water, drain, and let stand 20 minutes. Peel and slice crosswise about ¼-inch thick.

2. Trim the asparagus so that the tips are approximately 4 inches long. Tie the asparagus tips in a bundle with kitchen string and cook in boiling, salted water until tender, 10-20 minutes depending on the size of the asparagus. Cool under running water, remove the string, and drain on paper towels.

3. While the potatoes and asparagus are cooking, place the eggs in a saucepan with enough cold water to cover. Bring the water to a boil, turn down the heat, and simmer 10-12 minutes. Cool under running water and peel.

4. Rinse the romaine and watercress and trim off the stems and any bruised leaves. Shake the water off the leaves and wrap in a kitchen towel. Hold in the refrigerator.

5. Wipe the mushrooms with a damp paper towel. Trim the stems and slice about ¼-inch thick.

6. Cut the avocado in half lengthwise, remove the pit, and release the pulp from the shell in one piece. Slice each half lengthwise into 6 strips, place in a bowl, and sprinkle with lemon juice. Cover the avocado with plastic wrap to prevent discoloration.

7. Assemble the remaining ingredients.

MAYONNAISE DRESSING
8. Place the egg yolk, a pinch of salt, a few grindings of pepper, the mustard, and half of the lemon juice in a bowl. Stir with a whisk until well blended.

9. Add the oil a very small amount at a time, stirring continuously with the whisk. When the sauce begins to thicken and take on a lighter color, the oil may be added in a steady stream.

10. The mayonnaise is ready when it will hold in the whisk. Taste and season with salt, pepper, and the remaining lemon juice. Whisk in a small amount of oil to regain the right consistency.

11. Finish the mayonnaise by gradually stirring in enough cream to reach a smooth, sauce-like consistency. Blend in the paprika. Do not refrigerate.

FINAL ASSEMBLING
12. Tear the romaine lettuce and place it around the bottom of a large serving plate. Place the watercress around the outside edge. Put the alfalfa sprouts in the center on top of the romaine.

13. Overlap alternating slices of potato and mushroom in a ring around the outer edge on top of the watercress.

14. Place the asparagus in two bundles at ends of the plate inside the potato/mushroom ring. Slice the eggs and place them, overlapping, in the center of the plate between the asparagus spears. Place the olives around the egg slices.

15. Evenly space the avocado slices around the outer edge of the plate just beyond the potato/mushroom slices. Place a cherry tomato half in the center of each avocado slice.

16. The salad should be served at table with the dressing passed on the side.

Angel Food Cake With Strawberry Sauce

ANGEL FOOD CAKE
1½ cups egg whites (12-13 eggs)
1 cup cake flour
1½ cups granulated sugar
¼ teapoon salt
1½ teaspoons vanilla extract
1 tablespoon confectioners' sugar

STRAWBERRY SAUCE
1 quart strawberries
⅓ cup granulated sugar
1 tablespoon cherry liqueur
¼ cup red currant jelly

ANGEL FOOD CAKE
1. Let the egg whites come to room temperature before using.

2. Sift the cake flour and ½ cup of the sugar together 3 times.

3. Preheat the oven to 350 degrees.

4. Beat the egg whites in a copper or stainless steel bowl with a wire whisk. When the egg whites are frothy, add the salt and continue beating until the egg whites form soft peaks when the whisk is removed.

5. Sift the remaining 1 cup of sugar, 2-3 tablespoons at a time, over the egg whites. Beat the egg whites for 10-15 seconds after each addition to be sure that the sugar has been incorporated. When all the sugar has been added, continue to beat until the egg whites hold a stiff peak when the whisk is removed.

6. Fold in the vanilla extract. Sift the sugar/flour mixture, about ¼ cup at a time, over the egg whites. Fold in the dry ingredients after each addition just until well blended. Be careful not to overwork the batter.

7. Pour the batter into an ungreased 10-inch tube cake pan. Gently cut through the batter with a spatula to break any large air bubbles and smooth out the top.

8. Bake for 40-45 minutes or until the top of the cake springs back when lightly touched. Hang the cake, upside down, over a funnel for about 1 hour until it is cool. Loosen the cake from the pan with a metal spatula and turn the cake out onto a cooling rack. Sieve confectioners' sugar over the top and transfer to a serving plate.

STRAWBERRY SAUCE
9. Dip the strawberries in cold water for a second, remove the stems and any bruised spots, and drain thoroughly. Set aside 10-12 berries for decoration.

10. Purée the remaining strawberries with the sugar in a blender. Strain the mixture through a fine sieve to remove the seeds.

11. Bring the cherry liqueur and currant jelly to a boil in a saucepan, making sure that the jelly is dissolved. Stir in the strained strawberry purée and bring to a boil once again. Chill thoroughly.

DECORATION
12. Place the reserved strawberries in the center tube of the cake.

13. Pour a small amount of strawberry sauce over each piece as it is served. Pass the remaining sauce at table.

June Menu

Chicken in lemon sauce
Tomatoes Nicoise
Blueberry tart

Chardonnay

Dinner for six

Contrasts are important in the June menu. The mild lemon flavor and creamy quality of the chicken is an excellent foil for the sharp taste and colorful appearance of the tomatoes Nicoise. The blueberry tart highlights the meal with its crisp sugar crust, soft custard filling, and fresh fruit topping.

Chicken In Lemon Sauce

6 chicken breast halves, boned and skinned
¼ cup all-purpose flour
salt and freshly ground white pepper
4 tablespoons butter
1 tablespoon peanut oil
4 shallots, finely minced
grated rind and juice of 1 large lemon
½ cup dry white wine
¾ cup heavy whipping cream

1. Dust the chicken breasts with flour, salt, and pepper.

2. Place 2 tablespoons of butter and the oil in a sauté pan over medium heat, add the chicken breasts, and cook until nicely browned on both sides. Sauté a few breasts at a time and when done remove to a side dish.

3. Add the shallots to the sauté pan and cook over low heat until soft but not browned.

4. Add the rind, lemon juice, and wine and bring to a boil, scraping the bottom of the pan with a wooden spoon. Return the chicken breasts to the pan and simmer, covered, for 20-25 minutes or until tender but not falling apart. When the chicken breasts are cooked, remove them to a serving platter, leaving the sauce in the pan.

5. Stir the cream into the sauce over low heat and cook until the sauce has reduced and thickened somewhat. Taste and season with salt and pepper if necessary. Spoon the sauce over the chicken breasts. Serve immediately.

Tomatoes Nicoise

½ cup long grain rice
1 cup water
½ teaspoon salt
6 tomatoes
3 scallions, finely minced
1 tablespoon finely minced parsley
1 tablespoon finely minced fresh basil
     or 1 teaspoon dry basil
1 tablespoon capers
2 tablespoons chopped black olives
1 small green pepper, finely diced
1 tablespoon Dijon mustard
1 tablespoon mayonnaise

GARNISH
1 small head leaf lettuce
3 black olives, halved

1. Place the rice, water, and salt in a heavy-bottomed saucepan that has a tight-fitting lid. Uncovered, bring the water to a boil and cook until the water is no longer visible on the surface of the rice. Cover, reduce the heat to the lowest simmer, and cook for 12 minutes. Remove from the heat and let the rice dry out in the covered pan for 5 minutes.

2. Cut the tops off the tomatoes and scoop out the seeds and some of the pulp. Lightly salt the tomatoes and turn them upside down on paper towels to drain.

3. Put the scallions, parsley, basil, capers, chopped black olives, and green pepper in a bowl. Mix in the cooked rice and bind the ingredients together with the mustard and mayonnaise. Both the tomatoes and the stuffing may be held at this point until ready for service.

4. Preheat the oven to 350 degrees.

5. Place a portion of the stuffing in each tomato and put on a baking sheet. Bake in the oven for 5 minutes.

6. Serve the tomatoes on a plate lined with rinsed and trimmed leaf lettuce. Garnish each tomato with a black olive half, cut side down.

Blueberry Tart

SUGAR CRUST
7 ounces (1¾ cups) pastry flour
4 ounces (½ cup) butter, chilled
¼ cup granulated sugar
½ teaspoon salt
1 egg

CUSTARD FILLING
2 cups whole milk
6 egg yolks
¾ cup granulated sugar
⅓ cup all-purpose flour
1 vanilla bean*

BLUEBERRY DECORATION
1 pint blueberries
¼ cup granulated sugar
2 tablespoons water

SUGAR CRUST
1. Sift the flour into a chilled bowl. Cut the butter into quarters and then into ½-inch pieces. Add the butter to the flour in the bowl, and using the fingertips as scoops, toss the mixture to coat the butter with flour.

2. Working very quickly, pick up a quantity of the butter and flour and press the butter pieces between fingertips and thumbs, breaking the butter into smaller pieces. Drop the butter and flour that remains in the fingertips and again pick up another quantity, repeating the process until the size of the butter pieces has been reduced to ¼-½ inch in diameter.

3. Add the sugar and salt and toss to blend. Lightly beat the egg and add it to the flour also. Toss and mix the dough with the fingertips until the dough can be worked into a ball.

4. Place the dough on a work surface and do the final blending of flour, butter, and sugar by smearing the dough across the surface with the heel of the hand, a small quantity at a time. Gather the dough together and repeat this process.

5. Shape the dough into a smooth, flattened round, wrap in wax paper, and chill in the refrigerator 45-60 minutes. The dough will also keep in the refrigerator for several days.

6. Lightly dust both sides of the dough with flour and place on a lightly floured work surface. Roll out the dough starting in the center and working to the edges. Turn the dough as necessary to keep a round shape. Dust with a small amount of flour if the dough begins to stick to the rolling pin or work surface. When finished the dough should be about 3/16-inch thick.

7. Roll the dough up on the pin and unroll over an 8-inch tart or pie pan. Lift the dough to settle it in the bottom of the pan. Lightly press the dough around the sides of the pan. Be careful, the dough will tear easily.

8. Trim the crust and crimp the edges.

9. Preheat the oven to 400 degrees.

10. Cut a circle of wax paper 2 inches larger than the baking tin. Place the wax paper on the dough, pressing it around the sides. Weight the paper with raw rice or beans. Bake in the oven for 20 minutes.

11. Remove the crust from the oven and lift out the wax paper and weights. Reduce the temperature to 350 degrees, return the dough to the oven, and bake 10 minutes or until the crust is lightly browned. Cool the shell before filling.

CUSTARD FILLING
12. Put the milk and vanilla bean in a heavy-bottomed saucepan over medium heat and bring to a boil. Remove from the heat.

13. Beat the egg yolks and sugar in a mixing bowl until very pale yellow. Add the flour and mix thoroughly to form a smooth paste.

14. Slowly stir the milk into the egg/sugar mixture. Clean the saucepan and pour the mixture into it. Do not remove the vanilla bean. Place over medium heat and stir the mixture with a wooden spoon until it boils and becomes thick. Be sure to scrape the sides and bottom of the saucepan.

15. Remove from the heat and pass the custard through a fine sieve into a bowl. Cover the surface with plastic wrap and put in the refrigerator about 2 hours until the custard has cooled thoroughly.

BLUEBERRY DECORATION
16. Dip the blueberries in cold water and pick over them to remove any bruised or underripe berries. Drain on paper towels.

17. Fill the pastry shell with the cooled custard, smoothing out the surface. Completely cover this with blueberries, gently pressing them into the custard.

18. Place the sugar and water in a small saucepan over low heat. Stir until the sugar has dissolved and wash down the sides of the pan with water. Let the syrup boil for 1 minute.

19. Lightly brush the surface of the blueberries with the sugar syrup to give them a glaze. Refrigerate 2-4 hours before serving.

*If a vanilla bean is unavailable, add 2 teaspoons of vanilla extract just before the custard is passed through a sieve in step 15.

July Menu

Green pepper salad
Cheese soufflé
Frozen raspberry mousse

Zinfandel

Supper for four

Uncomplicated tastes seem well suited for the heat of the summer, and the bite of a roasted green pepper salad followed by the sharpness of a cheddar cheese soufflé is indeed refreshing. The spotlight, however, is on the fresh red raspberries. They are a rare treat worth savoring in the early part of July.

Green Pepper Salad

6 large green bell peppers
1 small garlic clove
salt and freshly ground black pepper
5 tablespoons olive oil
1 tablespoon lemon juice
2 whole pimientos
8 black olives

1. Preheat the oven to 400 degrees. Put the peppers directly on the middle rack in the oven and remove them as soon as dark spots begin to appear on the skin.

2. Rinse the peppers in cold water and rub off the skin. Drain on paper towels.

3. Crush the garlic clove with 1 teaspoon salt and a little pepper in a small dish. When a paste has formed, add the oil in a thin stream, blending with a whisk. Finally, whisk in the lemon juice.

4. Cut the peppers in half and remove the seeds and pulp. Cut the peppers lengthwise into strips a little less than a ½-inch wide. Arrange the peppers on a serving plate.

5. Slice the whole pimientos lengthwise into ¼-inch strips. Decorate the top of the green peppers with the pimientos and black olives.

6. Pour the dressing over the peppers. Let the flavors blend at room temperature for at least half an hour.

Cheese Soufflé

3 tablespoons butter
3 tablespoons all-purpose flour
1 cup milk
½ pound sharp Cheddar cheese, grated
salt and cayenne pepper
6 eggs, separated
1 tablespoon finely grated Parmesan cheese

1. Melt the butter in a heavy-bottomed saucepan. Stir in the flour, making sure no lumps remain, and cook gently for a couple of minutes.

2. Off the heat, add the milk to the saucepan and mix well. Return to medium heat and cook the sauce until it thickens and begins to bubble. Stir constantly, scraping the bottom and sides of the pan with a wooden spoon.

3. Over low heat, add the grated Cheddar cheese and stir until it has melted and the sauce is thick and smooth.

4. Add a pinch of salt and a dash of cayenne pepper. Beat again and remove from the heat.

5. Add the egg yolks, one at a time, stirring after each addition until well blended.

6. Preheat the oven to 375 degrees. Butter a 2-quart soufflé dish and dust with the Parmesan cheese.

7. While the sauce is cooling, beat the egg whites in a copper or stainless steel bowl until they are glossy and stiff. Do not beat so long that they dry out.

8. Stir a whisk-full of the egg whites into the sauce to lighten it then pour the lightened sauce over the remaining egg whites. Fold in just until blended. It is better to leave small clumps of egg whites than to overwork the batter.

9. Pour the mixture into the soufflé dish and bake in the oven for 30 minutes. To test if it is done, give the dish a slight shove. If the top crust moves slightly it is ready; if it trembles cook another 5 minutes. The soufflé must be served as soon as it is taken from the oven.

Frozen Raspberry Mousse

⅓ cup water
½ cup granulated sugar
1 vanilla bean*
4 egg yolks
1 pint raspberries
1 cup heavy whipping cream

1. Place the water, sugar, and vanilla bean in a saucepan over low heat. Stir until the sugar has dissolved, brush down the sides of the pan with water, then bring to a rolling boil over high heat. Set aside for 20 minutes and remove the vanilla bean.

2. Put the egg yolks in a copper or stainless steel bowl. Set over low heat and gradually beat in the sugar syrup. Continue beating the mixture until it is very pale yellow, has expanded in volume, and just begins to form soft peaks. This will take 10-15 minutes.

3. Remove from the heat and beat until the mixture is cool.

4. Do not rinse the raspberries. Reserve 8 to 12 depending on size and purée the remainder through a food mill. Fold the raspberry purée into the egg batter.

5. Whip the cream until it just begins to stiffen and form peaks. Fold this into the batter also.

6. Pour the mousse into parfait or bulb-shaped wine glasses and freeze for at least 3 hours. At serving time garnish each with 2 or 3 raspberries.

*If a vanilla bean is unavailable, add 2 teaspoons of vanilla extract along with the raspberry purée in step 4.

August Menu

Black pepper steak
Potato salad with string beans
Peaches in peach cream sauce

Cabernet Sauvignon

Dinner for four

Green string beans, especially when very tiny and freshly picked, are one of the finest summer vegetables. They are especially good when added to new potatoes in a lightly dressed salad. The mild salad is countered by the pungency of the pepper steak, and the meal is topped off with fresh peaches in a smooth sauce of cream cheese and peach purée.

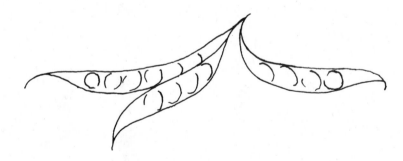

Black Pepper Steak

4 strip steaks (about 10 ounces each), cut 1-1½ inches thick
2 tablespoons black peppercorns, freshly cracked
*2-3 tablespoons clarified butter ***
2 tablespoons finely minced shallots
⅓ cup cognac
2 tablespoons butter

1. Brush both sides of the steak with clarified butter and cover with the cracked peppercorns. Push the peppercorns into the steak with the heel of the hand. Let the steak stand for 1 hour or longer so that the pepper flavor can be absorbed by the meat.

2. Heat a heavy-bottomed skillet just large enough to hold the steaks without crowding them. Use two pans if necessary. Brush the pan lightly with clarified butter and when it is very hot put in the steaks.

3. Sauté on one side for 4 minutes or until beads of moisture have formed on the surface of the meat. Turn and sauté on the other side for 4 minutes or until beads appear again. The steak will be medium rare when the meat begins to show some resistance and spring when it is touched.

4. Remove the steak to a hot platter and season with salt. Keep warm.

5. Pour the fat out of the skillet. Add 1 tablespoon of clarified butter and the shallots to the pan. Cook slowly for 2-3 minutes, scraping the bottom of the pan with a wooden spoon. The shallots should be soft but not browned.

6. Pour in the cognac, scrape the pan again, and reduce the sauce by half.

7. Off the heat, swirl in the 2 tablespoons of butter. Pour the sauce over the steaks and serve immediately.

*For a description of clarified butter, see step 2 of the recipe for rolled chocolate cake.

Potato Salad With String Beans

SALAD
6 small new potatoes
½ pound tiny string beans
3 small tomatoes
2 teaspoons granulated sugar
1 small head leaf lettuce

DRESSING
1 tablespoon lemon juice
1 teaspoon Dijon mustard
2 tablespoons finely chopped fresh basil
    or 1 teaspoon dry basil
2 tablespoons finely chopped parsley
salt and freshly ground white pepper
½ teaspoon granulated sugar
⅓ cup heavy whipping cream

SALAD
1. Cook the potatoes in boiling, salted water for 10-15 minutes until barely tender. Cool under running water, drain, and let stand 20 minutes. Peel and cut the potatoes in quarters.

2. Snap the ends off the string beans and cook uncovered in boiling, salted water about 7 minutes or until just tender. Cool under running water and drain.

3. Quarter and seed the tomatoes. Place in a bowl and toss with the sugar. Let the tomatoes stand 15-20 minutes then pour off and discard the accumulated liquid.

4. Rinse and trim the leaf lettuce. Shake off any moisture, wrap in a kitchen towel, and hold in the refrigerator.

DRESSING
5. Thoroughly blend the lemon juice, mustard, and seasonings in a small bowl. Let stand 15 minutes.

6. Slowly whisk in the cream. Taste and correct the seasoning if necessary.

7. Place the potatoes, beans, and all but 4 tomato quarters in a bowl. Whisk the dressing and pour over the salad. Gently toss the ingredients.

8. Line a serving dish with the leaf lettuce and cover with the salad ingredients. Decorate with the reserved tomato quarters.

Peaches In Peach Cream Sauce

4 tablespoons butter, softened
1 cup granulated sugar
12 ounces cream cheese, softened
½ cup sour cream
6 medium freestone peaches

1. Place the butter in a bowl and gradually beat in the sugar.

2. When the butter/sugar mixture is smooth and fluffy, beat in the cream cheese 4 ounces at a time. Beat the mixture after each addition of cream cheese until it is free of lumps.

3. Stir in the sour cream. The sauce may be held in the refrigerator at this point covered with plastic wrap. Bring to room temperature before continuing.

4. Bring a large saucepan of water to a boil and drop in the ripe peaches. Remove the pan from the heat and let the peaches rest in the hot water for 30 seconds. Cool the peaches under running water and drain. Peel the peaches, cut in half, and remove the pits.

5. Coarsely chop 6 peach halves and purée through a food mill. Blend the puréed peaches into the sauce.

6. Pour half of the peach cream sauce into 4 bulb-shaped wine glasses or other individual serving dishes. Place a peach half, rounded side down, in each glass and pour the remaining sauce on top, covering the peaches.

7. Slice the remaining peach into 16 sections. Decorate each glass with 4 peach sections, arranged pinwheel fashion, on top of the sauce. Chill 2-4 hours before serving.

September Menu

Roast pork with prunes
Pan-roasted potatoes and carrots
Apple Charlotte

Sauvignon Blanc

Dinner for six

With September, thoughts once again turn to more substantial meals. The roast pork with its surprise prune center and the pan-roasted potatoes and carrots are filling without being heavy. Apples, now ready for picking, are always a good accompaniment to pork. This time they appear in the dessert, an apple Charlotte.

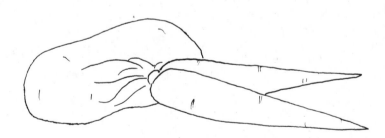

Pork Roast With Prunes

14 pitted prunes
2 cups dry white wine
3½-4 pound boned and tied pork loin roast
salt and freshly ground black pepper
2 tablespoons butter
1 tablespoon peanut oil
bouquet garni of
    3 parsley sprigs
    1 teaspoon dried rosemary

1. Soak the prunes in ½ cup of the white wine for 30 minutes.

2. Make a tunnel through the center of the pork loin roast with a long, sharp tool. A knife sharpening steel, a large metal knitting needle, or a larding needle work fine.

3. Stuff this tunnel with the softened prunes, packing them in with the handle of a wooden spoon. Rub the roast with salt and pepper.

4. Preheat the oven to 375 degrees.

5. Place the butter and oil in a casserole just big enough to hold the roast. Over medium heat brown the roast on all sides.

6. Remove the roast from the casserole and discard the fat. Return the roast to the pan and add the wine, bouquet garni, and any remaining juice from the prunes.

7. Cover the casserole and cook in the oven for 1½ hours or until the juice runs clear when the meat is pierced with a kitchen fork.

8. Remove the roast from the casserole and discard the bouquet garni. Degrease the pan juices and reduce the sauce over medium heat. Taste and correct the seasoning.

9. Remove the string from the roast and transfer to a serving platter. Carve the meat into 1-inch slices. A small amount of sauce may be served with the roast with the remainder passed at table.

Pan-Roasted Potatoes And Carrots

18 tiny new potatoes
10 medium carrots
1½-2 cups peanut oil
6 tablespoons butter
salt and freshly ground white pepper
pinch of thyme

1. Peel and carve the potatoes into the shape of a medium egg. If tiny potatoes are unavailable, quarter and trim larger ones. Rinse the potatoes in cold water and drain on paper towels.

2. Peel the carrots and cut into 1½-inch lengths. Save the narrow ends for another purpose and carve the remaining sections into oval shapes also. Dry the carrots on paper towels.

3. Add enough oil to cover a heavy-bottomed sauté pan by ¼ inch. Heat until quite hot, add the potatoes and carrots, and cook uncovered over medium heat, turning occasionally.

4. Remove the carrots as soon as they begin to turn golden and drain on paper towels. Continue cooking the potatoes, turning occasionally, until they are golden on all sides also. Remove and drain on paper towels. Pour off the oil.

5. Heat the butter in the sauté pan until foaming and add the potatoes. Cover the pot tightly and cook 20-25 minutes over low heat. Shake the pan every 5-10 minutes so that the potatoes cook on all sides.

6. When the potatoes can be easily pierced with a fork, add the carrots and season with salt, pepper, and thyme. Cook, covered, another 5 minutes to heat the carrots. Remove the vegetables to a serving dish with a slotted spoon.

Apple Charlotte

8 cooking apples
6 tablespoons butter
1 lemon
3 tablespoons granulated sugar
4 tablespoons apricot jam
14 slices of white bread, crusts removed
1 cup heavy whipping cream
2 tablespoons confectioners' sugar

1. Quarter, pare, and core the apples. Cut into ¼-inch slices.

2. Melt 4 tablespoons of butter in a large saucepan and add the apples. Cook over a medium heat until all the juices are released and the liquid in the bottom of the saucepan begins to boil.

3. Using a vegetable peeler, remove the very outer, yellow portion of the lemon in long strips and add to the saucepan. Squeeze the juice of the lemon into the pan also and stir in the sugar. Cook until the mixture begins to hold together, looking almost like applesauce.

4. Remove from the heat, take out the lemon rind, and stir in the apricot jam.

5. Preheat the oven to 400 degrees.

6. Generously butter a 1-quart charlotte mold.

7. Cut 4 slices of bread on the diagonal and trim into smaller triangles. Cut 8 slices of bread in half lengthwise. Place the triangles around the bottom of the pan and stand the halves up along the sides in an overlapping fashion. Cut a round of bread to fit the top of the mold. Two half circles may be used if necessary.

8. Pour the apple mixture into the mold and pack it down.

9. Butter one side of the round of bread for the top of the mold. Place the buttered side down on the apples.

10. Bake in the oven for 50 minutes.

11. Place the cream and sugar in a chilled bowl and beat until it stiffens and forms soft peaks. Transfer to a serving dish and hold in the refrigerator.

12. Remove the charlotte from the oven and let rest for 15 minutes before unmolding on a serving plate. Pass the sweetened whipped cream at table.

October Menu

Beef Stroganoff
Egg noodles
Pears with chocolate sauce

Pinot Noir

Dinner for six

As the weather cools, menus become more refined. Here the egg noodles are a tender bed for the Stroganoff which blends rare, sautéed beef filet in a gently seasoned cream sauce. Pears, at their prime, are draped with chocolate sauce and make a very pleasing finish for this dinner for six.

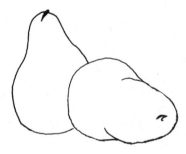

Beef Stroganoff

1 tablespoon powdered mustard
1 tablespoon granulated sugar
salt and freshly ground black pepper
1 tablespoon hot water
4 tablespoons peanut oil
2 medium onions, very thinly sliced into rings
1 pound mushrooms, trimmed and thinly sliced
2 pounds filet of beef, trimmed and cut into ¼ by 2 inch strips
1 pint sour cream

1. Combine the mustard, sugar, salt, pepper, and hot water in a small bowl. Mix to form a smooth paste.

2. Heat 2 tablespoons of the oil in a skillet. Add the onions and mushrooms, stir, and cook over medium heat until the moisture that the vegetables will release has all evaporated and the vegetables are soft. Transfer to a plate.

3. Heat 2 more tablespoons of the oil in the skillet and, over medium high heat, sauté a portion of the meat until lightly browned. Do not crowd the meat in the pan and cook only long enough to seal the outside. The meat should remain rare. Transfer the meat to a plate and cook the remaining pieces, transferring them also.

4. Add the mustard paste to the skillet and stir over low heat. Add the sour cream and blend thoroughly. Add the meat, mushrooms, and onions and cook until the meat and vegetables are warm and the sour cream begins to bubble. Do not let it boil.

5. Taste for seasoning and serve.

Egg Noodles

2 cups all-purpose flour
1 egg
4 egg yolks
1 teaspoon salt
1 tablespoon peanut oil
3-4 tablespoons water
4 tablespoons butter

1. Place the flour in a mixing bowl. Make a well in the center and add the egg, egg yolks, salt, oil, and 3 tablespoons of the water.

2. Begin combining the egg and oil with the flour using the flat side of a fork and folding the flour over the egg and oil. When well mixed begin working the dough with the fingers. Add small amounts of water as necessary to form a soft ball of dough.

3. Knead the dough lightly on a floured work surface 5-10 minutes until it is smooth and shiny. If the dough is sticky, dust lightly with flour and continue kneading.

4. Cover the dough with plastic wrap and let rest for 20 minutes.

5. Flatten the dough and dust both sides with flour. Place on a floured work surface and roll the dough out into a paper-thin circle, turning occasionally and flouring both the dough and the work surface to prevent sticking. The dough may also be divided in two and worked separately.

6. Let the dough dry out for 10-15 minutes. Lightly dust the dough once again with flour. If the dough has been divided into two pieces, roll up each piece and cut crosswise into even strips ¼-inch wide. If the dough was not divided before rolling, cut this large circle into two strips, stack them, roll up lengthwise, and cut into even strips ¼-inch wide.

7. Toss and unroll the uncooked noodles to separate them and let dry on the countertop at least 15 minutes.

8. Bring a large pot of water to a boil and add 1 tablespoon of salt. Shake any excess flour off the noodles and drop them into the boiling water. Cook 3-4 minutes. Pour into a large colander, quickly rinse with warm water, and drain thoroughly.

9. Melt the butter in the large pot, add the noodles, and toss to coat them with the butter.

Pears With Chocolate Sauce

PEARS
6 ripe pears
juice of half a lemon
¼ cup chopped dates
¼ cup chopped pecans
2 cups granulated sugar
1 cup water
½ vanilla bean
    or 1 teaspoon vanilla extract

CHOCOLATE SAUCE
3 ounces semisweet baking chocolate, broken in pieces
2 tablespoons butter
1 tablespoon cherry liqueur
¼ cup syrup from the poached pears

PEARS
1. Peel the pears leaving the stem attached. Remove the core from the base of each pear with a vegetable peeler. Place the pears in a bowl and sprinkle with the lemon juice.

2. Thoroughly mix together the dates and pecans. Place a portion of this mixture in the cavity of each pear.

3. Bring the sugar, water, and vanilla bean or extract to a boil in a medium saucepan. Brush down the sides of the pan with water and boil for 5 minutes. Add the pears, reduce the heat, cover, and simmer for 8-10 minutes, turning the pears 2 or 3 times in the process. Poach the pears in two batches if necessary. They should not be crowded in the pan.

4. Cool the pears in the syrup and then drain on paper towels. Strain the syrup through a fine sieve and reserve ¼ cup for the chocolate sauce.

CHOCOLATE SAUCE
5. Place the chocolate, butter, and liqueur in a heavy-bottomed saucepan over low heat. Stir to blend the mixture thoroughly and remove from the heat as soon as the chocolate has melted.

6. Add the strained poaching syrup a little at a time, stirring the sauce until it reaches a thick pouring consistency.

DECORATION
7. Place the drained pears in a serving bowl with the stems up. Pour a small amount of the hot chocolate sauce over each pear to coat the stem and begin draping the sides. Pass the remaining sauce at table.

November Menu

Scallops in cream sauce with rice
Bibb lettuce salad
Rolled chocolate cake

Dry Chablis

Dinner for six

Scallops are a change of pace from the poultry and fowl traditionally served in November. The main course is substantial, combining shellfish, vegetables, and rice, and should stand alone. The salad serves to clear the palate between the entrée and the splendid rolled chocolate cake.

Scallops In Cream Sauce With Rice

RICE
1½ cups long grain rice
3 cups water
pinch of salt
1 tablespoon butter

SCALLOPS IN CREAM SAUCE
6 tablespoons butter
6 small carrots, cut in julienne
3 small celery ribs, cut in julienne
8 medium mushrooms, sliced
salt and freshly ground white pepper
½ cup dry white wine
½ cup water
1½ pounds scallops
2 egg yolks
1 cup heavy whipping cream
2 teaspoons Dijon mustard
3 tablespoons all-purpose flour
juice of half a lemon

RICE
1. Place the rice, water, salt, and butter in a heavy-bottomed saucepan that has a tight-fitting lid. Leave uncovered, bring the water to a boil, and cook until water is no longer visible on the surface of the rice.

2. Cover, reduce the heat to the lowest simmer, and cook for 20 minutes.

3. Remove from the heat and let the rice dry out in the covered pan for another 10-20 minutes.

SCALLOPS IN CREAM SAUCE
4. Melt 3 tablespoons of butter in a large saucepan. Add the carrots and celery and simmer, covered, about 10 minutes or until the vegetables are barely tender.

5. Add the mushrooms, a little salt and pepper, and the white wine and simmer uncovered for 4-5 minutes or until the mushrooms become limp. Remove the vegetables with a slotted spoon to a side dish.

6. Add the water to the liquid in the saucepan, bring to a boil, and add the scallops. Simmer, covered, for 5 minutes. Drain the scallops and reserve the poaching liquid. Hold the scallops in a warm spot.

7. While the vegetables and scallops are cooking, put the egg yolks, cream, and mustard in a small bowl. Whisk until thoroughly blended.

8. Melt the remaining 3 tablespoons of butter in the saucepan, blend in the flour thoroughly, and cook for 3-4 minutes over medium heat.

9. Measure 1 cup of the poaching liquid and stir it into the saucepan. Cook, stirring constantly, over medium heat until the sauce is smooth and bubbling. Taste and add salt, pepper, and all or part of the lemon juice as necessary.

10. Gradually stir in the cream/egg yolk mixture and heat briefly to let the sauce thicken. Do not let it boil or the egg will curdle.

FINAL ASSEMBLING
11. Spoon the rice onto a serving platter and place the scallops on top.

12. Stir the vegetables into the hot sauce and pour over the scallops and rice. Serve immediately.

Bibb Lettuce Salad

2 medium heads bibb lettuce
1½ tablespoons tarragon wine vinegar
salt and freshly ground white pepper
6 tablespoons olive oil

1. Trim and rinse the lettuce. Shake off the excess moisture, tear the leaves as necessary for serving, and wrap in a kitchen towel. Place the lettuce in the refrigerator to crisp.

2. Put the vinegar, salt, and pepper in a small bowl and stir to dissolve the grains of salt. Gradually blend in the olive oil.

3. Place the lettuce in a serving bowl. At table, pour the dressing over the salad, toss gently, and serve immediately.

Rolled Chocolate Cake

CHOCOLATE CAKE
4 eggs, at room temperature
½ cup granulated sugar
1 teaspoon vanilla extract
½ cup cake flour
⅓ cup unsweetened cocoa powder
6 tablespoons butter

CHOCOLATE BUTTER CREAM
6 ounces semisweet baking chocolate, broken in pieces
2 tablespoons water
1 pound butter, softened
1 cup granulated sugar
½ cup water
8 egg yolks

CHOCOLATE CAKE

1. Lightly butter a 10 by 15 inch jelly roll pan. Line with buttered wax paper and dust with cocoa powder.

2. Place the butter in a small saucepan over low heat. When it has melted, remove from the heat and skim off and discard the white foam on the surface. Pour the yellow portion of the melted butter into a small dish. Discard the white residue at the bottom of the pan. The butter is now clarified.

3. Sift the flour and cocoa together 3 times.

4. Preheat the oven to 350 degrees.

5. Put the eggs in a copper or stainless steel bowl. Gradually beat in the sugar and then the vanilla. Continue beating for 20-25 minutes until the egg mixture has thickened, is shiny, and falls from the whisk in a ribbon pattern.

6. Sift the cocoa/flour mixture over the eggs, about ¼ cup at a time, folding after each addition just enough to blend.

7. Continue to fold the batter while slowly pouring in the clarified butter. Fold just until the butter has blended in.

8. Pour the batter into the greased pan and spread it evenly with a spatula.

9. Bake for 10-12 minutes or until the cake springs back when touched. Do not let the edges of the cake dry out.

10. While the cake is baking, dust a clean kitchen towel with a little cocoa powder. When the cake is done, let it cool 15-20 minutes before turning it out, upside down, on the towel. Remove the pan and wax paper. Let the cake finish cooling with a slightly damp kitchen towel draped over it.

CHOCOLATE BUTTER CREAM

11. Melt the chocolate with the water in a small heavy-bottomed saucepan over low heat. Stir often and remove from the heat just before the chocolate has completely melted.

12. Beat the softened butter until it is light and fluffy.

13. Put the sugar and water in a heavy-bottomed saucepan over low heat. Stir until the sugar has dissolved then brush down the sides of the pan with water. Over high heat cook the syrup until it begins to spin a thread or has reached the jelly stage (220 degrees) on a candy thermometer.

14. Whisk the sugar syrup into the egg yolks in a steady stream. Continue beating until the mixture is thick and cool. It will fall from the whisk in a ribbon pattern.

15. Gradually beat in the whipped butter. Continue beating until the butter cream is thick and holds its shape.

16. Finally, beat in the cooled chocolate. Chill until the butter cream is the right consistency before spreading on the cake.

FINAL ASSEMBLING

17. When the cake is completely cool, remove the cloth and spread the cake with a thick layer of the butter cream. Roll the cake up starting at the short end and turn it so that the seam is on the bottom.

18. Place the cake on a serving plate and decorate the outside of the cake with the remaining butter cream. The cake should be held in the refrigerator until serving.

December Menu

Oyster stew
Yeast rolls
Plum pudding with hard sauce

Brut Champagne

Supper for four

The December menu features warm and comforting foods. Oyster stew — especially with fresh shucked oysters — is a delicacy. The yeast rolls and plum pudding seem to melt in the mouth. What better way to soothe a year-end spirit.

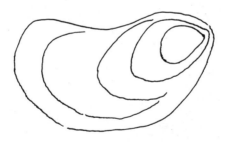

Oyster Stew

1½ cups whole milk
1½ cups heavy whipping cream
salt and freshly ground white pepper
grating of nutmeg
4 tablespoons butter
2 dozen oysters (about 1½ pints, shucked)

1. Thoroughly scrub the oysters under running water.

2. Place the oyster in a hand protected by a pot holder, glove, or dish towel. Put the point of an oyster knife, can opener, or ice pick in the hinge and push in to open. Slide the blade of the oyster knife in at this opening and draw it around the edge where the two half shells meet, opening the oyster and severing one of the muscles that attaches the oyster to the shell. Separate the other muscle from the shell. Place the oyster and its juice in a bowl and discard the shells.

3. Bring the milk, cream, salt, pepper, and nutmeg to a simmer in a heavy-bottomed saucepan or double boiler.

4. Melt the butter in a sauté pan and when it is foaming add the oysters and their juice. Cook 2-3 minutes until the edges of the oysters ruffle.

5. Add the oysters and the juice to the milk and heat for a minute. Serve immediately.

Yeast Rolls

1 cup milk
1 tablespoon granulated sugar
1 package yeast
4-5 cups unbleached all-purpose flour
2 teaspoons salt
½ cup butter, softened
2 eggs, lightly beaten

GLAZE
1 egg
1 tablespoon milk

1. Warm the milk in a small saucepan. When 80-90 degrees for compressed yeast or 110-115 for dry, add the sugar and yeast. Let it soften for a few minutes, then stir to dissolve.

2. Place 2 cups of flour and the salt in a large mixing bowl. Add the yeast mixture and stir with a wooden spoon until the batter is smooth. Beat in the butter and then the eggs.

3. When the batter is once again smooth, add 2 more cups of flour and mix, with a wooden spoon and then with the hands, until a rough dough is formed. Add a little more flour if the dough remains sticky.

4. Turn the dough out onto a lightly floured work surface. Knead 5-8 minutes until the dough is smooth and elastic. When necessary, dust the work surface with additional flour to keep the dough from sticking.

5. Place the dough in an ungreased bowl. Cover the bowl with plastic wrap and set in a warm spot to let the dough rise until doubled in bulk. At about 85 degrees this will take 2-2½ hours.

6. Punch down the dough and knead very lightly for a minute. Divide the dough into 3-ounce pieces, cover with plastic wrap, and let rest 3-4 minutes.

7. Shape each piece into a ball by working the dough on a counter under a cupped hand, using a circular motion. As the rolls are formed, place them on baking sheets lined with cooking parchment paper.

8. To glaze the rolls, lightly beat the egg and milk together. Gently brush each roll with the glaze.

9. Let the rolls rise about 1 hour or until they have doubled in size.

10. Preheat the oven to 400 degrees. Bake 15-20 minutes until a golden crust has formed on the surface and the bottom is hard when tapped.

Plum Pudding With Hard Sauce

PLUM PUDDING
¼ cup candied citron, chopped
¼ cup candied lemon peel, chopped
1 cup golden raisins, chopped
1 cup currants
½ cup all-purpose flour
4 ounces beef suet, grated
½ cup packed light brown sugar
1½ cups loose fresh breadcrumbs
½ cup blanched almonds, chopped
½ teaspoon ground cinnamon
½ teaspoon grated nutmeg
¼ teaspoon ground ginger
½ teaspoon salt
½ teaspoon baking powder
¼ cup milk
2 eggs
¼ cup cognac
grated rind of 1 lemon
1 tablespoon lemon juice

HARD SAUCE
⅓ cup butter, softened
1 teaspoon vanilla extract
1 cup confectioners' sugar

PLUM PUDDING
1. Place the citron, lemon peel, raisins, and currants in a large mixing bowl and dust with the flour.

2. Add the suet, brown sugar, breadcrumbs, almonds, cinnamon, nutmeg, ginger, salt, and baking powder. Stir to blend well.

3. Add the milk and eggs and mix thoroughly.

4. Finally, stir in the cognac, grated lemon peel, and lemon juice. This batter may be kept in the refrigerator for one week or longer to blend the flavors.

5. Butter the bottom and sides of a 1-quart mold and pour in the batter. The refrigerated pudding mixture should be stirred thoroughly before filling the mold. If the mold does not have a hinged lid, cover the top with lightly buttered aluminum foil and tie it securely to the mold.

6. Lower the mold onto a trivet or rack in the bottom of a pot that is about 4 inches larger in diameter than the widest part of the mold. Pour in enough boiling water to come half way up the side of the mold. Cover the pot and place over low heat for 2 hours. The water should boil gently all the time that the pudding is steaming. Add boiling water, if necessary, to keep at the same level.

7. The pudding may be refrigerated in its mold after it has cooked and cooled. To reheat before serving, steam the pudding, as in the preceeding directions, for 30-45 minutes.

8. Loosen the pudding from the baking tin with a metal spatula and unmold onto a serving plate.

HARD SAUCE
9. Cream the butter in a small bowl until light yellow and fluffy.

10. Add the vanilla extract and the sugar and beat until this is fluffy also. The hard sauce may be refrigerated. Bring to room temperature and beat before transferring to a serving dish. Pass the sauce at table.

INDEX

Angel food cake with strawberry sauce, 31
Apple Charlotte, 50
Apricot sauce, Pineapple with, 19
Artichokes stuffed with lump crabmeat, 23

Bavarian cream, Chocolate, 13
Beef Burgundy, 6
Beef Stroganoff, 52
Bibb lettuce salad, 57
Black pepper steak, 44
Blueberry tart, 36
Bread, Country white, 11
Butter cream, Chocolate, 58

Cake
   Angel food with strawberry sauce, 31
   Rolled chocolate, 58
Carrot soup with cabbage, Purée of, 10
Carrots and potatoes, Pan-roasted, 49
Charlotte, Apple, 50
Cheese soufflé, 41
Chicken in lemon sauce, 34
Chicken, Roast, with sautéed cherry
   tomatoes, 16
Chocolate Bavarian cream, 13
Chocolate butter cream, 58
Chocolate cake, Rolled, 58
Chocolate sauce, Pears with, 54
Country white bread, 11
Crabmeat, lump, Artichokes
   stuffed with, 23
Crêpes Suzette, 24
Cucumber and yogurt soup, 28

Grand Marnier soufflé, 8
Green pepper salad, 40

Hard sauce, Plum pudding with, 64

Mayonnaise, 29
Mousse, Frozen raspberry, 42

Noodles, Egg, 53

Oyster stew, 62

Peaches in peach cream sauce, 46
Pears with chocolate sauce, 54
Pineapple with apricot sauce, 19
Plum pudding with hard sauce, 64
Pork roast with prunes, 48
Potato puffs, 18
Potato salad with string beans, 45
Potatoes and carrots, Pan-roasted, 49
Potatoes, Buttered, 7

Raspberry mousse, Frozen, 42
Rice, 56
Roasts
    Chicken with sautéed cherry
        tomatoes, 16
    Pork with prunes, 48
Rolled chocolate cake, 58
Rolls, Yeast, 63

Salad
    Bibb lettuce, 57
    Green pepper, 40
    Potato with string beans, 45
    Spring, 29
Scallops in cream sauce with rice, 56
Soufflé, Cheese, 41
Soufflé, Grand Marnier, 8
Soup
    Cucumber and yogurt, 28
    Oyster stew, 52
    Purée of carrot with cabbage, 10
    Vichyssoise, 22
Steak, Black pepper, 44
Strawberry sauce, Angel food cake with, 31

Tart, Blueberry, 36
Tomatoes, cherry, Sautéed, 16
Tomatoes, Nicoise, 35

Yeast rolls, 63
Yogurt soup, Cucumber and, 28

Vichyssoise, 22